This bite-sized
useful overvie
to achieve the

- ✓ Understan
- ✓ Be more considered and well-structured in your responses
- ✓ Take an analytical and objective approach
- ✓ Distil complexity and be a better problem-solver
- ✓ Save time through smarter thinking

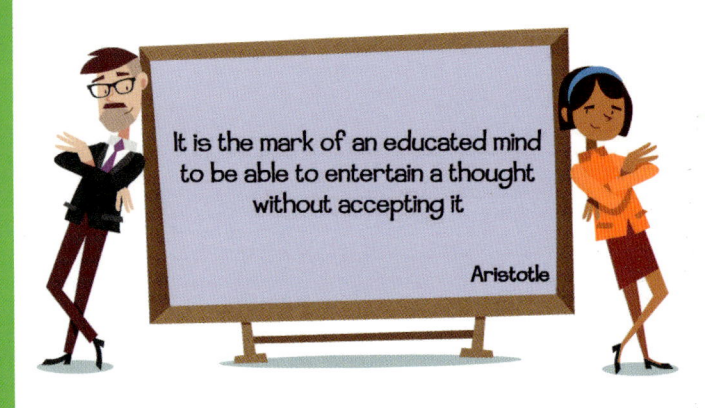

> It is the mark of an educated mind to be able to entertain a thought without accepting it
>
> Aristotle

What is critical thinking?

Critical thinking is about distilling and processing information, distinguishing fact from fiction, and applying rational judgement to real-world situations. In simple terms, it is about thinking clearly and carefully so we can arrive at well-reasoned conclusions instead of just accepting everything at face value. Critical thinking involves skills like analysing, interpreting, evaluating, questioning assumptions and validity, identifying biases and considering different perspectives.

The aim of critical thinking is to be objective, logical, well-informed and open-minded in deciding what we believe and do with information. Critical thinking also helps us to distil complexity so we can be better communicators, decision-makers and problem-solvers. Essentially, this way of thinking helps us to actively and skilfully make better sense of the world around us.

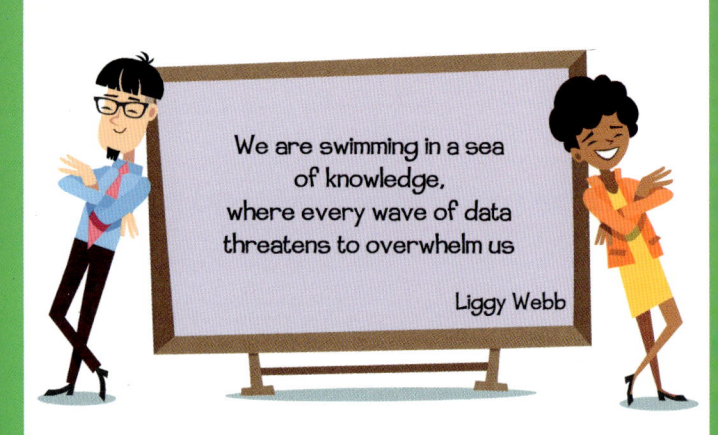

> We are swimming in a sea of knowledge, where every wave of data threatens to overwhelm us
>
> Liggy Webb

Information anxiety

Do you ever feel overwhelmed with all the information that is out there?

Information anxiety is a recognised term that refers to the feeling of stress and overwhelm caused by the ever-increasing gap between the information we understand and the information we feel we should understand. This discomfort can arise from an overload of data, coupled with the feeling that we are constantly falling behind on what we think we 'should' know.

Critical thinking is crucial for mitigating information anxiety because it helps us to analyse and process complex information with clarity and confidence. Critical-thinking skills can also have a positive impact on our wellbeing by helping us to navigate information overwhelm and reduce any fear we may have of being misled by misinformation.

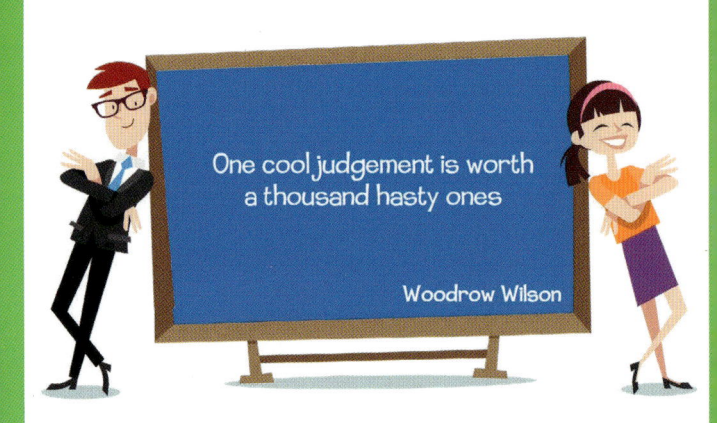

> One cool judgement is worth a thousand hasty ones
>
> Woodrow Wilson

Respond well

When it comes to critical thinking, the distinction between being responsive and reactive is crucial. Being reactive is often initiated by an immediate problem, challenge or question. We may feel a tendency to jump to conclusions or solutions without thoroughly analysing the situation. These reactions might be influenced by personal biases, assumptions, pressure from others or immediate feelings rather than objective analysis.

Responsive thinking, however, involves taking the time to understand the situation fully before formulating a response or solution. This is a way of thinking that examines the issue from multiple angles, breaks it down into its component parts and evaluates the available information. Responsive critical thinking strives to minimise the influence of personal biases and emotions by focusing on evidence and evaluating a range of possible solutions before choosing the most appropriate one.

> When we blindly adopt a religion, a political system, a literary dogma, we become automatons
>
> Anais Nin

The origin of critical thinking

The term 'critical thinking' originates from the Greek word 'kritikos', meaning 'able to judge or discern'. The history of critical thinking can be traced back to the ancient philosophers, particularly Socrates and Aristotle, who emphasised the value of questioning and examining assumptions. Socrates' method of probing questioning exposed the lack of rational justification for many beliefs, highlighting the importance of questioning authority and assumptions. This is a type of open-ended inquiry that is designed to encourage deep thinking and self-reflection.

There are many benefits to critical thinking and here are a few examples:

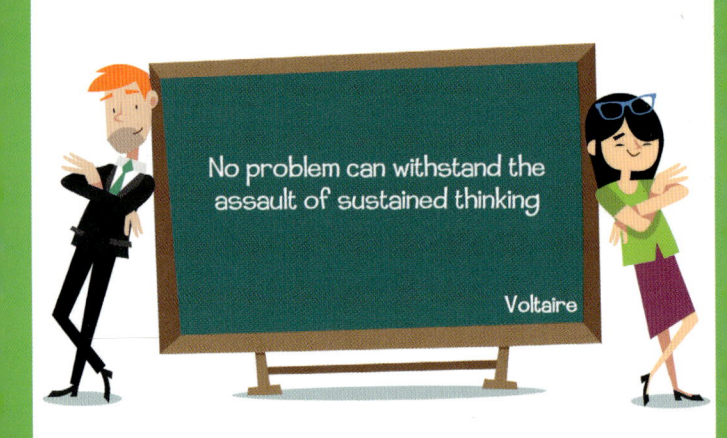

> No problem can withstand the assault of sustained thinking
>
> Voltaire

Smarter thinking

Critical thinking is about smarter thinking and is a highly valuable and important employability skill. It is not just about being able to think logically and analyse information, it is about applying those skills to real-world situations and problem-solving in both our personal and professional lives.

Critical thinking will also help us to keep exploring and learning in a quest for fresh information. Knowing how to distil complexity by filtering out the irrelevant information from the relevant is a key time-saver. Critical thinking will also help us to prioritise our time and resources by analysing what is essential to the process. Smarter thinking carries a wealth of benefits that will touch various aspects of our lives, leading to greater effectiveness, overall wellbeing and personal growth.

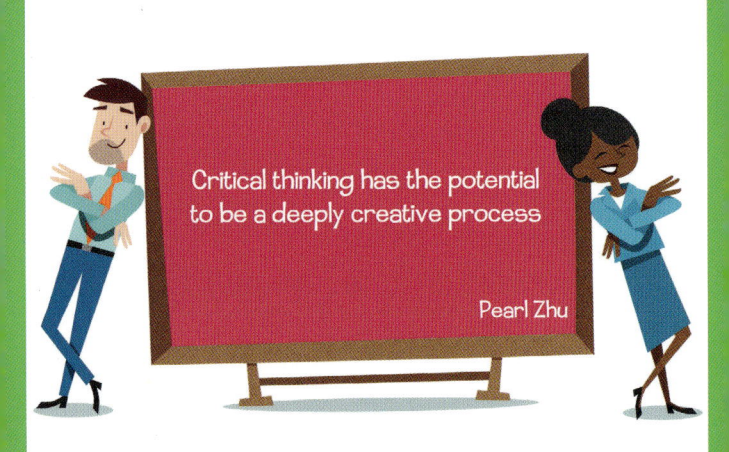

> Critical thinking has the potential to be a deeply creative process
>
> Pearl Zhu

Complex problem-solving

Critical thinking is indispensable for tackling complex problems and equips us with the ability to dissect multifaceted issues into smaller, manageable components. This allows for a more systematic and thorough analysis which will help us to move beyond surface-level understandings so we can uncover the root causes of complex problems.

Critical thinking also fosters the generation of innovative and adaptable solutions. Instead of relying on conventional approaches, critical thinking encourages us to explore alternative perspectives and challenge established norms. By logically evaluating the potential outcomes of different strategies and anticipating potential challenges, we can make better informed decisions about which solutions are most likely to succeed.

Improved credibility

Critical thinking can elevate our credibility by ensuring that our communication is well-founded and logically sound. By rigorously evaluating information, identifying biases and constructing coherent arguments, we can present viewpoints that are demonstrably more reliable. This careful approach to forming and expressing our ideas signals competence and helps us to be more persuasive and believable.

Critical thinking also nurtures intellectual honesty and open-mindedness. When we demonstrate a willingness to consider different perspectives and acknowledge the limitations of our own knowledge, we are viewed as dependable and trustworthy, which can strengthen our credibility.

The next few pages share a variety of practical tips on how to be a critical thinker.

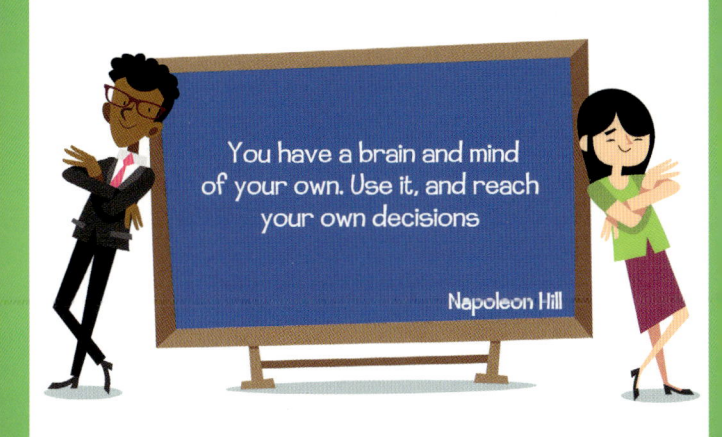

> You have a brain and mind of your own. Use it, and reach your own decisions
>
> — Napoleon Hill

How to think critically

Take time to think

Taking time to think is a crucial element when applying critical thinking. It allows for a deeper and more thorough analysis of information rather than jumping to immediate conclusions. Taking time to think fosters a more open-minded approach, which is essential for effective critical thinking. It provides the space to challenge initial assumptions and explore alternative interpretations.

This reflective period allows us to connect new information with existing knowledge, identify inconsistencies, and evaluate the strength and relevance of different arguments. Without this deliberate pause, critical thinking can become rushed and superficial, increasing the likelihood of errors in reasoning and less robust conclusions. It pays to remember that the sharpest insights aren't forged in haste, but in the quiet space of timely and considered thought.

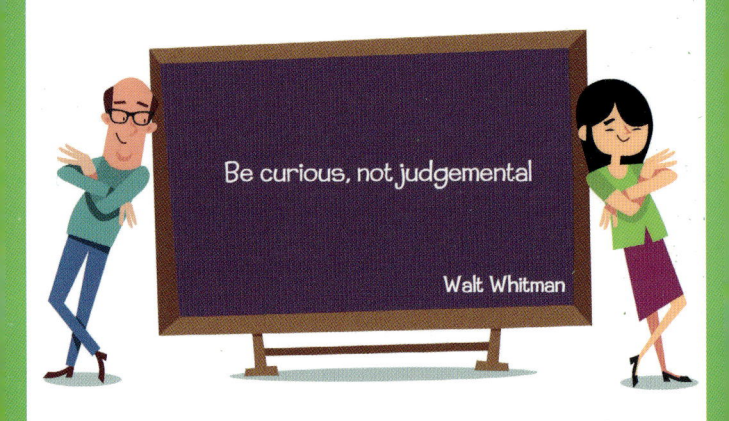

Be curious, not judgemental

Walt Whitman

Be curious

Curiosity acts as the spark that ignites the engine of critical thinking and when we are curious, we actively seek out new information, explore different perspectives and question existing assumptions. Curiosity helps us to understand things better and compels us to dig deeper, rather than accepting surface-level explanations.

Curiosity encourages us to be more open and receptive, which is essential for objective analysis and evaluation. When we are curious, we are more likely to approach new ideas with intrigue rather than being immediately dismissive of something. By constantly seeking knowledge and challenging our own understanding of it, curiosity cultivates the intellectual flexibility and analytical rigour that is required for critical thinking.

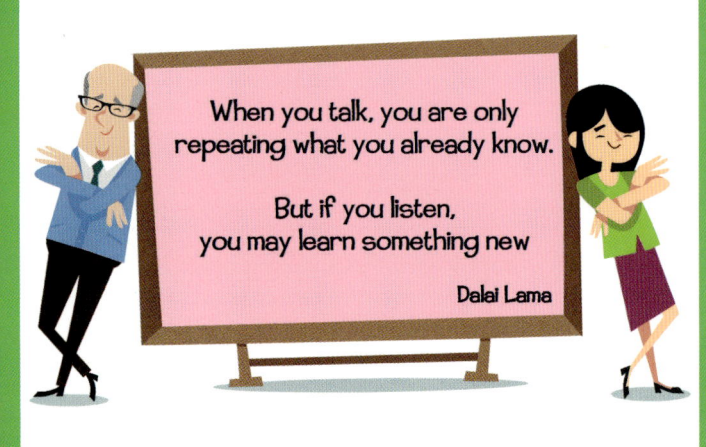

When you talk, you are only
repeating what you already know.

But if you listen,
you may learn something new

Dalai Lama

Observe and listen

Observation is one of the earliest critical-thinking skills we learn and this is about our ability to perceive and understand the world around us. When we carefully observe and document details, we will be able to collect information and gain better insight and a deeper understanding of each situation.

Listening is a cornerstone of critical thinking because it provides the raw material for analysis and evaluation. When we deeply listen, it helps us to identify key arguments, detect inconsistencies and understand the context in which information is presented. Without carefully listening, we risk misinterpreting information, overlooking crucial details and forming judgements based on incomplete or inaccurate understandings.

The important thing is
not to stop questioning

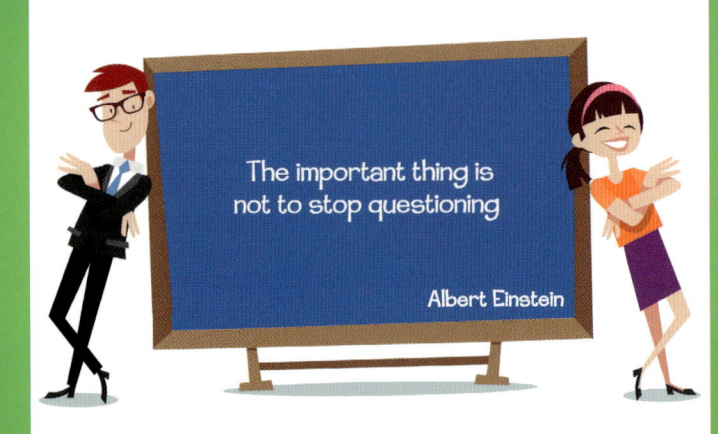

Albert Einstein

Probe and question

To probe for critical thinking, ask open-ended questions that require more than a simple 'yes' or 'no' answer. Questions that start with Who, What, When, Where, Why and How are all good for probing for more information.

Here are a few examples of probing questions:

- What evidence do you have to support your claim?
- How reliable is that evidence?
- Who was involved in this research?
- What are the potential consequences of this decision?
- How does this information connect to what we already know?
- What makes this situation similar to or different from other situations we have encountered?
- What further information would be helpful to evaluate this more thoroughly?
- Why did you come to that conclusion?

Be analytical

Being analytical is about breaking information down into component parts and evaluating how well those parts function together and separately. Analytical thinking begins with objectivity and relies on us observing, gathering and evaluating evidence so we can arrive at a better-informed and more meaningful conclusion.

To become more analytical, it helps us to focus on identifying the underlying structure and meaning of information. Instead of just accepting facts at face value, we need to question their validity, connections and implications. We need to seek out supporting evidence, consider alternative interpretations and evaluate the reliability of the information sources.

Interpret and evaluate

We live in a world where fake news and misinformation is rife. It can take on various forms, including fabricated stories, manipulated content or out-of-context information. The aim is often to deceive, influence opinions or even cause harm.

To interpret and evaluate effectively for critical thinking, we need to delve into the material we are presented with, actively noting and questioning its claims. It also helps to consider perspectives, potential biases and the overall purpose of the information. We can then identify any logical flaws and evaluate the strength and credibility of our evidence. This will help us to formulate a more reasoned and confident opinion, rather than just accepting the information.

Don't raise your voice,
improve your argument

Desmond Tutu

Manage emotions

Critical thinking and staying calm really do go hand-in-hand. When we approach situations with a clear and cool head, our ability to analyse information, evaluate different perspectives and make sound judgements significantly improves.

If we are stressed or overwhelmed by emotions like fear and anger, our minds won't be as clear or receptive. When we are calm, we can process information more effectively, consider different viewpoints without getting defensive or raising our voices, and avoid making rash decisions. When we feel strong emotions arising, deep breathing, progressive muscle relaxation and taking time to rest or get some fresh air can all be helpful.

> A great many people think they are thinking when they are merely rearranging their prejudices
>
> William James

Understand your default bias

Critical thinking is essential for identifying and mitigating our unconscious biases and autopilot responses. These biases are ingrained assumptions and stereotypes that operate outside our conscious awareness and can significantly twist our judgement and lead to unfair or irrational opinions.

Understanding our unconscious biases requires a deliberate effort to become aware of our ingrained assumptions and how they might influence our thoughts and actions. Critical thinking plays a crucial role in this self-awareness by encouraging us to reflect on our past decisions, identify patterns in our judgements, and actively seek out diverse perspectives that challenge our existing beliefs. By engaging in this process of critical self-reflection and actively considering alternative viewpoints, we can begin to recognise the influence of our unconscious biases. This will help to lead us to more thoughtful and unbiased responses instead of relying on our automatic 'autopilot'.

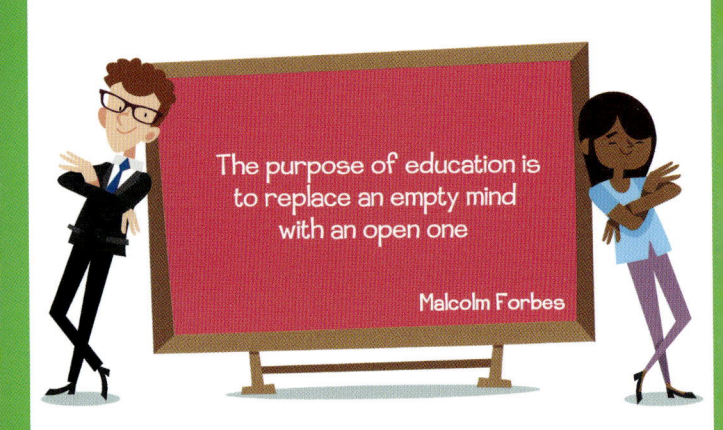

> The purpose of education is to replace an empty mind with an open one
>
> Malcolm Forbes

Keep an open mind

Keeping an open mind is fundamental to critical thinking because it allows us to move beyond our pre-existing beliefs. When we approach information or arguments with a willingness to consider different perspectives, we create space for new evidence. This openness enables us to evaluate information more objectively, identify potential flaws in our own reasoning, and ultimately arrive at better conclusions. Without an open mind, critical thinking becomes constrained by our current understanding, limiting our ability to learn and grow.

An open mind also encourages intellectual humility, because we recognise that our current knowledge is not absolute and that others may hold valuable insights. This encourages us to actively seek out diverse viewpoints and consider different angles, which will help us to avoid the pitfalls of narrow-mindedness and fixed thinking. Embracing open-mindedness truly enriches the critical-thinking process, leading us to more robust and insightful analyses.

Be willing to challenge

Challenging information and applying critical thinking are essential for navigating a world saturated with diverse and often conflicting messages. By actively questioning claims, analysing evidence and evaluating the logic behind arguments, we can empower ourselves to discern reliable information from misinformation or manipulation.

Also, a willingness to challenge and think critically fuels innovation and progress. By questioning existing assumptions and exploring alternative perspectives, we can identify limitations in current knowledge and pave the way for new discoveries and solutions. A willingness to apply critical thinking encourages intellectual curiosity and continuous learning, which is essential in the constantly changing world that we live in.

In summary

Here is a five-step approach to critical thinking that summarises the content of this bite-sized book:

1. **Identify the problem** – Define the issue or question and understand the scope, context and potential implications

2. **Gather information** – Collect relevant data, evidence and information from various sources through research, experimentation, observation, or consulting with experts

3. **Analyse the information** – Examine the gathered information, identify patterns and evaluate its relevance and reliability. This step involves questioning assumptions, considering different perspectives and looking for inconsistencies or biases

4. **Draw conclusions** – Based on the analysis, formulate a reasoned conclusion or decision. This involves weighing up evidence, considering potential consequences and making a judgement about the best course of action

5. **Evaluate the decision** – Reflect on the decision, consider alternative outcomes, and assess the effectiveness of the chosen solution. This step involves learning from the process and identifying areas for improvement.

> Learn to use your brainpower. Critical thinking is the key to creative problem-solving in business
>
> Richard Branson

Recommended resources

These books and resources have been curated to help you to take a deeper dive into the concept of critical thinking.

- ✓ Thinking, Fast and Slow – Daniel Kahneman
- ✓ The Art of Thinking Clearly – Rolf Dobelli
- ✓ Critical Thinking – Tom Chatfield
- ✓ How to Think Like Socrates – Donald J. Robertson
- ✓ Parallel Thinking – Edward de Bono
- ✓ Black Box Thinking – Matthew Syed
- ✓ The Rules of Thinking – Richard Templar
- ✓ Critical Thinking Skills – Stella Cottrell
- ✓ Intelligent Thinking – Cathrine Kowal

If you would like a free copy of the digital poster on page 38 please email: liggy@liggywebb.com

CRITICAL THINKING
How to think clearly and rationally

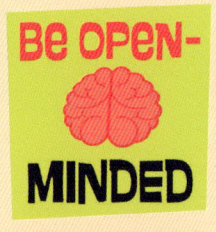

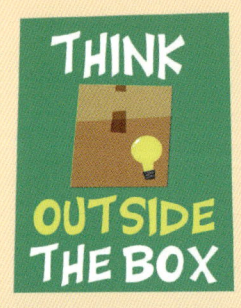

- CHALLENGE INFORMATION
- QUESTION THE SOURCE
- BE OPEN-MINDED
- Manage EMOTIONS
- ANALYSE INFORMATION
- Be CURIOUS
- LOOK FOR EVIDENCE
- THINK OUTSIDE THE BOX
- COMMUNICATE WITH CLARITY
- RESEARCH AND EXPLORE

One of the most powerful skills we all need to cultivate is the ability to think with critical objectivity

Liggy Webb

Explore more at: www.liggywebb.com